# Success with

# Begonias

## HALINA HEITZ

Series Editor:
## LESLEY YOUNG

MEREHURST

# Introduction

Begonias are magnificent colourful flowering plants and decorative foliage plants rolled into one – they can be grown for either their blooms or their greenery and are sure to capture the heart of any plant lover with their profuse displays of blossom.

This full-colour guide will introduce you to this extremely adaptable and versatile genus of plants, and will suggest many possibilities for using begonias indoors, on balconies or patios and in the garden. The comprehensive text has been written particularly for the newcomer to begonias but will be of equal interest to the enthusiast or passionate collector who is always on the lookout for botanical rarities.

In this guide, the author, herself an experienced plant grower, offers an introduction to the many beautiful begonias available for cultivating indoors and in the garden and provides botanical and gardening information, technical tips and easy-to-follow instructions on cultivation and care. There are many useful hints about buying begonias and you will also find all the necessary information on botany, care and propagating to keep your plants in good health. The splendid colour photographs, specially taken for this guide by Jürgen Stork, have been chosen to convey an impression of the profusion of colour and varied shapes of leaves and flowers to be found among begonias. Every year new cultivars appear on the market, each one more attractive than the one before. Shrub begonias, so beloved of the Victorians, and other exotic varieties are currently enjoying a widespread revival and most of these plants are now available on the market.

# Contents

*Begonia x gigantea bud.*

*Begonia acida from Brazil.*

*Like a rose-quartz necklace – the flowers of Begonia dichroa.*

### The author

Halina Heitz has also written plant guides to palms, orchids, roses and indoor plants. For fifteen years she was the editor in chief of a German specialist gardening magazine called *Mein schöner Garten.*

### Acknowledgements

The author and publishers wish to thank Josef Ruf and Murg and Karl Zwermann of Usingen-Wernborn for allowing them to photograph begonias in their nurseries. Our thanks also go to the college of gardening with ornamental plants in Weihenstephan, as well as to begonia raisers Benary, Rieger and Diener, French begonia raiser Claude Ferry and Patrick Rose of the Begonia Museum at Rochefort in France for their expert advice.

**Important:** Please make sure that you read the "Important note" on page 47.

# All about begonias

## An asymmetrical leaf – the begonia's key feature

According to the most recent scientific study of this subject, about 1,000 different species of begonias grow on our planet. Apart from a few exceptions, all have asymmetrical leaves, which have become almost a "trade mark" of the begonia species. This botanical family of plants owes its name to the Frenchman Michel Bégon.

### An introduction to the begonia family

The genus of begonias belongs to the family of the similar name, *Begoniaceae*, and there are only two other related genera, the genus *Symbegonia* and the genus *Hillebrandia*. Within the internationally accepted botanical classification system, *Begonia* is a member of the *Dicotyledonae* subclass of angiospermous plants; to be exact, it belongs to the First Class and Twenty-third Order of *Violales*. To date, botanists have been unable to find any ancient forms of this plant, which might have served as ancestors, so it is assumed that we are dealing here with a very "young" flowering plant that is still capable of evolving and that the chances of it becoming the precursor of new families of plants are high. According to the latest estimates, in addition to the thousand-plus species of begonias, there are approximately 15,000 hybrids.

### How the names evolved

As stated above, the main charac-teristic feature of the genus *Begonia* is its asymmetrical leaf, which means that one "half" of the leaf is a different size to the other. This feature is completely unique to begonias and does not appear in any other family of plants. The genus *Begonia* actually owes its name to the man who discovered fuchsias, Charles Plumier (1646-1704). He discovered several begonia species around 1690 and bestowed upon them the name of his travelling companion at the time, Michel Bégon (1638-1701) who was the governor of Santo Domingo. The name was first published by French botanist Pitton de Tournefort in his *Institutiones Rei Herbariae* in 1700.

### Where do begonias come from?

Begonias originated in the subtropical and tropical regions of the Americas, Africa and Asia. There are no wild begonias in Australia. Most of them grow in the tropical regions of South America, mainly in Brazil, the Amazon region, Bolivia and Peru, but also in the Andes of Ecuador and along the western chain of the Cordillera Real mountains as far south as the 35th parallel. Central America and Mexico are also known for their begonia species. Generally speaking, Asia ranks second as far as numbers of species are concerned, in particular, the eastern and central parts of the Himalayas, Sri Lanka, South-East Asia and China. The most northerly place in which begonias have ever been found is the area around China's capital city, Beijing. The tropical areas of Africa are rich in begonias. They can also be found in the humid regions of West Africa, in Cameroon and in the subtropical areas of Natal (South Africa). Finally, we must not forget to mention the arid island of Socotra (or Suqutra), east of the Gulf of Aden, which is where *Begonia socotrana*, the ancestor of our present-day foliage and tuberous begonias, originates. Most begonia species grow in warm, humid rainforests where they live near the ground, being shade-loving plants. Some of them have evolved into epiphytes and have colonized the branches and trunks of trees, other species prefer the breezy elevations of mountainous regions up to altitudes of 4,000 m (13,123 ft), while other species, again, love cool, arid regions. All of them, with very few exceptions, have a great preference for positions that receive plenty of light (providing they are semi-shady or out of direct sunlight), plenty of humidity and soil that is humus-rich, water-permeable and constantly moist and warm.

### Various kinds of growth

Begonias produce so many varieties that even botanists and gardeners have a hard time creating some kind of order in the classification system. You can find:
- shrubs or semi-shrubs;

- annual or perennial plants;
- creeping plants;
- climbing and hanging plants;
- epiphytes.

The smallest known begonia is *Begonia hymenophylla*. It grows no taller than 5 cm (2 in) and has small leaves only 6-9 mm (less than ⅜ in) long. The largest species is probably *Begonia arborescens*, a shrub that may attain a height of 2-3 m (up to 10 ft).

## Roots, rhizomes or tubers

Whereas some species of begonias have quite ordinary fine, fibrous, flat, spreading root systems, others form thick underground stems (rhizomes) which creep through the soil and form new roots at intervals. A third group produces, fleshy, thickened tubers, used for storing nutrients, at the ends of the stems.

*Begonias with ordinary root systems* are divided into three types.
1. Smooth shoots, fairly woody, with swellings or bulges in some places. The leaves are shaped like angels' wings, lobed at the tips and extremely asymmetrical. These plants form bushes or shrubs.
2. Fleshy shoots. Some parts of the plant, particularly the leaves and the flowers, are thickly covered with hairs. They usually grow into shrubs and are pendulous.
3. Fleshy shoots with waxy, hairless leaves.

*Begonias which form rhizomes* usually grow prostrate and rarely taller than 20-30 cm (8-12 in). Their leaves are particularly beautiful, almost circular, nearly star-shaped or heart-shaped. The flowers are fairly inconspicuous.

*Tuberous begonias* usually lose their foliage in autumn and enter a period of dormancy, although there is a group which only flowers in winter. These are the short-lived species which we tend to throw away after they have finished flowering.

*Begonia x gigantea, a rhizomatous begonia with bristly leaves and shoots.*

*Begonia metallica – even the flowerbuds are densely covered with hairs.*

## Shapes, colours and structures

The sheer variety of shapes, colours and patterns of leaves among begonias is almost inexhaustible – as you will see from the examples shown here. Individual leaves from the following species and varieties are depicted:

1.  "Beverly Jean"
2.  "Perle de Lorraine"
3.  "Silver Queen"
4.  *Begonia imperialis* "Speculata"
5.  *Begonia heracleifolia* "Fuscomaculata"
6.  *Begonia heracleifolia var. nigricans*
7.  *Begonia masoniana* "Iron Cross"
8.  "Cathedral"
9.  "Tiger"
10. *Begonia caroliniifolia*
11. "Sabi"
12. "Halina"
13. "Pearlii"
14. "Joe Hayden"
15. "Empereur"
16. "Guy Savard"
17. "Comtesse de Montesquieu"
18. *Begonia strigillosa*
19. "Bahamas"
20. "Amazing Lace"
21. "Spectrum"
22. variety of "Trush"
23. "Boomer"
24. "Bettina Rothschild"
25. "Bow-Arriola"
26. *Begonia acida*

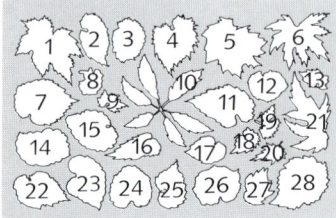

27. "Trush"
28. "Comtesse Louise Erdody"

*A nostalgic trip into the past: Begonia "Lucerna", a famous cultivar from the nineteenth century.*

### Stems, stalks and shoots

Have you ever wondered why begonia shoots are as brittle as glass and break off so easily? This is because they contain a great quantity of sap, are soft and fleshy and frequently very slender. However, there are other variations on this: species with hard, woody shoots or, as in the case of *Begonia caroliniifolia*, having almost gristly stems. Many species of begonias have smooth shoots, with swellings at intervals, so that they look a little like bamboo stems. For this reason,

these species are often referred to as "bamboo" begonias. Some species display hairy or even scaly stems (*Begonia acida*, see photo p. 19), are coloured purple (*Begonia sutherlandii*), or have a thick tuber at their base (*Begonia dragei*). *Begonia octopetala* has no stem at all, while *Begonia veitchii*, *Begonia davisii* and *Begonia paulensis* display short, thick stems.

### A great variety of leaves

(see photo, pp. 6/7)
Many species and varieties have

such attractive and unusual leaves that they have been classified as the "foliage" begonias (see pp. 12/13). The leaves grow on the stem in an alternating arrangement and are all asymmetrical. (Exceptions: *Begonia luxurians*, which has spear-shaped leaves arranged symmetrically, *Begonia venosa* with oval leaves and *Begonia baumannii* with broad/oval leaves.) They may be divided or undivided, depending on the species.

*Among the various shapes of leaves* can be found roundish, long, oval, reversed-oval and shield-shaped (peltate) variants. The leaf edges may be serrated, lobed, smooth, dentate or have hairs like eyelashes.

*The multitude of different structures and patterns found in the leaves* exceeds anything known in other plant families. The surfaces of the leaves may be hairy, granular, scaly, deeply furrowed, curly, bare on top, woolly on the underside or display a circle of small, dark red bristles. They may have a metallic gleam or may shine like silk, this being caused by the presence of light-reflecting cells in the epidermis.

*When it comes to the colours of its leaves*, Begonia has well nigh exhausted the range of colours found in nature. Ranging from white and silver grey to pink, red, purple, violet and brown right through to almost black, all colours are represented, and that is without mentioning the many different shades of green. You may also come across marbled, veined, spotted, dotted, striped and criss-cross effects.

*One botanical curiosity* is represented by the "hood-bearing" *Begonia hispida var. cucullifera* (see photo, p. 19). This variety forms tiny, ready-grown young plantlets on its leaves, a phenomenon that is duplicated in the plant kingdom by only one species of fern (*Asplenium viviparum*) and *Kalanchoe pinnata*. An amusing variant is the snail-shell-shaped leaf of the shrub begonia "Comtesse Louise Erdody" (see photo, p. 19).

## Metamorphic flowers

*Botanical data:* Begonias form false flower umbels which always grow out of the leaf axils. We refer to umbels as being "false" if individual flowers are clustered together but do not grow out of the same part of the plant. The male and female flowers appear on the same plant but in different places. The male flowers are usually equipped with two outer perianth segments and two inner ones, and the female flowers have five, occasionally two or eight, perianth segments. Both genders of flowers may appear on the same inflorescence – as a rule the female ones will grow at the end of the shoot (terminal) and the male ones along the sides of the shoot (lateral). There are also species in which the male and female parts form visibly separate inflorescences. The ovary is an unmistakable feature of female inflorescences, which appears as a three-lobed appendage immediately below the flower. The male flowers contain numerous stamens, arranged in several circles, and fairly large, conspicuous, yellow anthers. Female flowers last for several weeks but their colours fade after a few days, while the male flowers drop off after two to three days but have stronger colours.

*Shapes and colours:* This is probably the area in which the genus *Begonia* most clearly demonstrates its great versatility, leaving raisers plenty of room in which to experiment with ever-new hybridized creations. Even the wild species seem to display boundless variation: upright or nodding false umbels which resemble strings of opals, coral or rose quartz, in brilliant shades of yellow, orange and red, transparent pink, iridescent white and entrancing double colours. The only colours missing from the range are blue and violet. However, the complete palette is not really revealed until hybridizing occurs. Then one discovers flowers that look like roses (see photo, p. 21), buttercups (see photo, p. 14), anemones (see photo, p. 21), carnations, dahlias (see photos, p. 21 and 25), camellias or hibiscus flowers, and in colours with a brilliance that has hardly ever been attained by any other species of plant, especially among the tuberous begonias.

## Fruits and seeds

Begonias have a very distinctly shaped stigma and a winged ovary. In the wild, pollination takes place through the action of wind or insects. The fruit, a capsule that pops open when ripe, contains very small seeds – there may be as many as 60,000 to 70,000 individual seeds per gram of weight. The ripe seeds contain practically no nutrients, which explains the very short timespan during which begonia seeds are able to germinate.

## Are begonias toxic?

To date, no cases are known of the poisoning of humans or animals through eating any parts of begonia plants. Various toxic substances have been found in the tuberous begonia, *Begonia x tuberhybrida*, however, including oxalic acid (which is also found in rhubarb, spinach and sorrel) and cucurbitacin B in the subterranean parts. This suggests a certain similarity to, and possibly some relationship with, *Cucurbitaceae* (gourds).

In their countries of origin, begonias are used as astringents and cooling agents in skin care or as a sudorific (causing perspiration) or diuretic (causing an increase in urine). The leaves of some Asiatic species are eaten as a vegetable, for example, *Begonia edulis*. Finally, the acidic juices are reputed to be suitable for cleaning weapons! Discussions currently continue among specialists as to whether begonias have similar qualities to those of *Dieffenbachia* spp. and certain other species (known to produce irritants which affect the skin and mucous membranes).

# Begonias for indoors and out

Whichever you prefer most – the brilliant colours of the flowering begonias, the subtle charms of shrub begonias, the individual shades of the foliage begonias – the following pages will give you an opportunity to indulge yourself by reviewing a selection of attractive species and varieties for your home, balcony, patio or garden.

The classification of the following groups of begonias would not be considered quite correct according to the scientific/botanical viewpoint. In the USA, which has a long tradition of cultivating begonias, botanists have adopted a taxonomy that groups begonias according to growth, root systems, or hybrid group. According to Thompson & Thompson (authors of *Begonias – The complete reference guide*, published by Times Books, New York) the following groups have been established:

- shrub begonias;
- thick-stemmed or thick-shooting begonias;
- bamboo begonias;
- rhizomatous begonias;
- creeping, climbing and pendulous begonias;
- Rex begonias;
- tuberous begonias;
- Elatior begonias;
- Semperflorens begonias.

For most begonia enthusiasts, however, disagreements among scientists are of secondary importance. What the enthusiast wishes to know, above all, is which begonias are suitable for indoors or the garden and how to look after them. As no agreement has yet been reached on an internationally recognized taxonomy, for simplicity's sake, we recommend that you stick with the old, fairly well-known division. It is a rough system but one that gives a reasonable overview.

**Foliage begonias** are particularly conspicuous on account of their beautiful leaves. They usually have rhizomes.

**Flowering begonias** are treasured for their attractive flowers and profusion of blooms. This group includes the Elatior and Lorraine begonias, the Semperflorens begonias and tuberous begonias.

**Shrub begonias** are plants with shoots that turn woody, thick or even cane-like.

All groups incorporate pendulous, creeping and climbing species and varieties and other intermediate types. This means that some foliage begonias produce enchantingly beautiful flowers, while the foliage of some flowering begonias is also quite unusual.

Certain differences are also distinguishable where care is concerned. As proper care is the be-all and end-all of growing healthy begonias, this aspect is covered for each group so that you can see at a glance how to treat each specimen. The list of begonias that follows begins with representatives that are ideal for indoors and ends with varieties that are more suitable for outside. The section entitled "Begonias for collectors" is not a special group that is particularly difficult to care for but merely a small selection of especially interesting or rare species and varieties. The begonias are introduced in the following sequence:

- foliage begonias (see pp. 12/13);
- Elatior begonias (see pp. 14/15);
- shrub begonias (see pp. 16/17);
- begonias for collectors (see pp. 18/19);
- tuberous begonias (see pp. 20/21);
- Semperflorens begonias (see pp. 22/23).

*Tips on care* include individual details about positioning, soil, watering, fertilizing, repotting and propagating.

*"My tip"* draws on the author's own experience to give particular advice or recommendations.

*A dream in pastel pink*
*Pink is the basic colour, firmly established in the genes of all Elatior begonias, which appears in a whole range of different shades.*

*Begonia masoniana "Iron Cross" is named for its leaf markings which resemble the old German medal.*

**A wonderful variety of shapes and patterns**

# Foliage begonias

Striking colours, patterns and shapes are the hallmark of the foliage begonias, which usually produce rhizomes. Among this group, flowers are of less importance.

*Position:* Light, but not too sunny, semi-shady. Rex hybrids should be kept at an even temperature all year round (never below 20°C or 68°F), while other species and varieties

may be kept a little cooler. Provide humidity but do not mist. In the case of Rex begonias, provide indirect humidity. Stand the pots in a bed of moist peat, on a warm, humid windowsill with other plants, or place the pots on a tray of constantly moist Hortag or sand. All other types can tolerate ordinary indoor air.

*Soil:* Standard compost, flower pot-

"Trush" leaves bear pink "pearls".

Begonia rex hybrids need plenty of warmth and humidity.

Begonia ricinifolia "Immense".

"Sabi" has silver-coated leaves.

Rex begonia.

A variation on Begonia boweri.

ting compost; mix in Perlite or polystyrene flakes.

**Watering:** Do this with a great deal of care. The rootstock should never be allowed to dry out, but neither should it be completely wet. Never wet the leaves. Reduce watering during the winter.

**Fertilizing:** From early spring to early autumn, every eight days,

sparingly – avoid waterlogging.

**Repotting:** Only in spring, if the root system has become very dense. If necessary, trim the rootstock. Shallow bowls are preferable.

**Propagating:** From cuttings, leaf or rhizome parts (see pp. 38-40).

**My tip:** Some foliage begonias lose older leaves, particularly if in a position that is too dark in winter. Stand

the plants in a place that is a little cooler and dryer, then they will enter a kind of dormancy period. They will grow new foliage in spring.

**Note:** If you are growing Rex begonias, pinch out any flowers that appear in the summer as they will use up energy which the plant should be devoting to the growth of leaves.

*Rieger's famous "Schwabenland".*

*Pink-flowering "Susi".*

*Benary's "Charisma", the first begonia cultivar to propagate from seed.*

*"Goldstar" has hibiscus-like blooms.*

*Edged in salmon pink: "Korona".*

*The vividly coloured "Renaissance".*

**Flowers all year round**

# Elatior begonias

These begonias are often bought as a "bouquet in a flowerpot", as they flower all year round and are sold at fairly reasonable prices.

**Position:** Light, but not in sunlight. Keep them at room temperature all year.

**Soil:** Commercial potting compost.

**Watering:** Give plenty of water if the rootstock is dry. Get rid of any surplus water to avoid "wet feet".

**Fertilizing:** Every fortnight with flower fertilizer.

**Repotting:** Not applicable. As this is a plant which forms flowerbuds in winter and new shoots in summer, further growth is only successful in conditions supplied by a nursery.

**Propagating:** Cuttings from shoot tips in early summer (see p. 39).

*"Alma" enchants with its pompon flowers in a fiery shade of orange and fascinating, jagged leaves.*

# Shrub begonias

This group includes perennials as well as semi-shrub types and shrub species and varieties that can be cultivated for years. They flower profusely and can climb, spread or form cane-like shoots. Most of them also display extremely attractive leaves.

*The flowers of Begonia metallica.*

The best known representatives of this group are the Corallina hybrids like "Lucerna" (see photo, p. 8), *Begonia limmingheana*, *Begonia serratipetala*, *Begonia metallica*, *Begonia egregia*, *Begonia* "Comte de Miribel" (see photo, p. 30) and other varieties of *Begonia coccinea* and *Begonia solananthera*. In addition, there are the very attractive *Begonia x gigantea* (see p. 5), *Begonia dichroa* (see p. 3), Begonia Gracilis hybrids, *Begonia bradei* and *Begonia foliosa var. miniata* (syn. *Begonia fuchsioides*).

### Care of shrub begonias

*Position:* Provide light all year round. In winter they may be placed in a sunny position but avoid the midday sun! Smooth-leaved species can tolerate more light and sunlight than species with hairy leaves.
***Temperature:*** In the summer 20-

*Begonia metallica has deep pink, down-covered flowers.*

*Begonia "Argenteo-guttata".*

*Begonia Corallina hybrid.*

*"Amazing Lace" has beautiful foliage.*

*Pearl white flowers on emerald green foliage: shrub begonia "Manuela".*

*The flowers of Begonia egregia from Brazil smell of mimosa.*

22°C (68-72°F); in winter a little cooler but never below 15°C (59°F).
**Soil:** Standard potting compost or azalea potting compost. Mix in polystyrene flakes to aerate the soil.
**Watering:** Always keep the rootstock at a constant degree of moistness. If there is waterlogging or if the rootstock dries out, the leaves may drop off.

**Fertilizing:** From early spring to late summer, every eight days to a fortnight, with flower fertilizer.
**Repotting:** Early spring to the middle of summer whenever necessary but it can also be done at other times of the year. Young plants can be repotted twice a year and older ones should be repotted if the rootstock has become very dense.

**Pruning:** In spring before repotting; pruning into shape can be done in the summer. Regularly remove the shoot tips on young plants.
**Propagating:** Cuttings from shoot tips will easily form roots (p. 39).
**My tip:** When repotting, mix both polystyrene flakes and a controlled-release fertilizer with the fresh compost.

# Begonias for collectors

If you are interested in the unusual or in collecting botanical rarities, you will find a number of interesting species and varieties among the begonia family.

● Begonia "Bettina Rothschild" stands out for the deep red colouring of its shoots – including the hairs. Another name for this upright-growing Rex begonia is "Fire Flush", and not for nothing! Care is the same as for foliage begonias (see pp. 12/13).

● *Begonia heracleifolia* In addition to dense hairs, this species displays leaves like those of the hogweed (*Heracleum sphondylium*), which are hand-shaped and have seven to nine divisions. Care is the same as for foliage begonias (see pp. 12/13).

● *Begonia hispida var. cucullifera* is the name of a begonia which produces tiny "hoods". On its leaves, small 3-cm (1¼ in) hood-like, adventitious leaflets are formed, which are really ready-grown young plantlets. Care is the same as for shrub begonias (see pp. 16/17).

● *Begonia* "Comtesse Louise Erlody" is a Rex begonia with spirally rolled-up leaves. Care is the same as for foliage begonias (see pp. 12/13).

● *Begonia acida* attracts attention with its large, vivid green, almost circular leaves. Care is the same as for shrub begonias (see pp. 16/17).

● *Begonia caroliniifolia* has thick, almost gristly shoots which can be encouraged to form right-angled growth by pruning them. For this reason, it is sometimes called the "bonsai begonia". Care is as for shrub begonias (see pp. 16/17).

*Red leaf shoots of Begonia "Bettina Rothschild".*

*The leaves of Begonia heracleifolia var. nigricans.*

*Begonia hispida var. cucullifera.*

*"Comtesse Louise Erdody".*

*Leaf of "Bettina Rothschild".*

*The striking leaves of Begonia acida.*

● *Begonia luxurians* is similar to a *Schefflera*, grows taller than 1 m (40 in) and produces large, white, sweet-smelling inflorescences. Care is as for shrub begonias (pp. 16/17).

● *Begonia goegoensis* originates from Sumatra and forms a short, thick rhizome and shield-shaped, almost circular, dark green leaves. The surface of the leaf is partially uneven and granular and is marked with a web of light green veins. The underside is brilliant red. The plant bears pink flowers and needs plenty of warmth. Care is as for foliage begonias (pp. 12/13).

● *Begonia* "Perle de Lorraine" is a Lemoine cultivar with striking foliage. The leaves are oval and pointed, asymmetrically heart-shaped and dark olive green on top with chocolate brown veins and red undersides. The plant forms upright pink inflorescences. Care is as for shrub begonias (see pp. 16/17).

● With its delicate foliage, *Begonia foliosa* makes a wonderful, deep green plant for hanging baskets. Care is the same as for foliage begonias (see pp. 12/13).

*A yellow-flowering pendulous begonia brings colour to a balcony and will not take up a lot of room.*

**Flowers in glowing colours**

# Tuberous begonias

These are perhaps the most loved of all begonia types as they put on such a wonderfully colourful show, even in less well-lit positions. Plants of different heights, with large or small flowers, as well as plants suitable for hanging baskets are all available, not to forget the sun-loving Bertinii begonias.

**Position:** Light to semi-shady.

Bertinii and Multiflora varieties can cope with sunny positions.

**Soil:** In boxes with standard potting compost or an ordinary flower compost, or in garden soil in flowerbeds.

**Watering:** On warm days, give them a thorough daily soaking. Make sure to let surplus water drain away. Water less from late summer

*A cultivar with anemone-like flowers.*

*The dainty "Bali Hi".*

*Benary's snow white "Memory".*

*"City of Ballarat", a fiery orange cultivar from Britain.*

*This tuberous begonia displays rose-like, double flowers.*

onwards and allow the plants to reduce their foliage from mid-autumn onwards.

**Fertilizing:** Weekly from spring until mid-autumn, so that the tuber can regenerate.

**Overwintering:** Take the boxes or pots indoors after the first frost. Cut back dried-up or frozen foliage or stems to 2-3 cm (¾-1¼ in) and care-fully shake the soil off the tuber. If it sticks, leave it, as the tuber must not become damaged. Store the tubers in a cool, dark place (5-10 °C/41-50°F) in airy, wooden boxes or baskets until they begin shooting again (see p. 36).

**Propagating:** By dividing the tuber.

**NB:** Some tuberous begonias sud-denly start producing single flowers in the autumn. This is only because the days are getting shorter. The following summer, they will produce double flowers again.

**My tip:** I leave my plants outside in the autumn until the first frost. Most varieties show a distinct increase in the growth of their tubers during the shorter autumn days.

*White Semperflorens hybrid, "Whisky".*

*A rare two-coloured cultivar – "Rum".*

*Flowers in a vivid shade of pink – "Tiefrosa Vision".*

*The Semperflorens begonia "Rote Vision".*

**Carpets of colour**

# Semperflorens begonias

You will find many varieties of Semperflorens begonias on the market today. There are varieties with green foliage and some with almost black foliage, some that grow short and low, as well as large-flowered varieties that grow to a height of 45 cm (18 in). The spectrum of flower colours ranges from white to various shades of pink and salmon pink to the deepest shades of red. The white-edged varieties are very attractive. The flowers may be single or double. Semperflorens begonias are generally grown as annuals and almost only ever as garden plants.

***Position:*** Flowerbeds, borders, plant troughs, balcony boxes in a light to sunny position.

*Semperflorens begonias look best covering large areas and in combinations of several shades of the same basic colour.*

**Planting out:** The end of spring.
**Soil:** Standard potting compost, flower compost. Mix polystyrene flakes with the compost. In a garden bed, loosen up heavy soil by adding peat and hygromulch.
**Watering:** Do not allow the soil to become too moist as the roots will then begin to decay. As a rule, rain showers during summer should be sufficient for Semperflorens begonias planted outside. The soil in boxes or large containers will tend to dry out rather more quickly, however, so plants in these situations will need watering on hot days.
**Fertilizing:** Every two to three weeks with a flower fertilizer.
**Repotting and overwintering:** This is not applicable as these begonias are usually grown as annuals.
**Pruning:** This can be done in summer after the first crop of flowers. The plants will form new shoots.
**Propagating:** From seed. Heating facilities and artificial lighting will be needed.

**My tip:** Deadheading will extend the flowering season.

# History and hybridizing

How did begonias develop their vividly coloured flowers and how did the foliage produce such fantastically varied patterns? This is due to the efforts of hybrid raisers in the nineteenth century, and to those who have continued to experiment with begonias to the present day.

**A brief history of the begonia**
The oldest depictions of begonias are to be found in Asia, where, from very early times, the Chinese used the indigenous "Autumn-Haitang" (presumably *Begonia sinensis*) as a motif when painting on porcelain. The Japanese likewise reproduced *Begonia discolor* (syn. *Begonia grandis*) on other exquisite works of art. It was not until much later that the American species were discovered and became widely known to botanists.
● 1577: discovery of *Begonia gracilis* under the Mexican name of Totoncaxoxo coyollin.
● 1690: creation of the generic name *Begonia* by Charles Plumier.
● 1695: description of *Begonia tuberosa* in the *Herbarium Amboinense*.
● 1700: establishment of the name by Pitton de Tournefort in his work *Institutiones Rei Herbariae*.
● 1753: the Swedish botanist Linnaeus described all species and varieties known at the time, according to his classification system, which is still in use today.
● 1777: Sir Joseph Banks exported *Begonia nitida* (syn. *Begonia minor*) from Jamaica to Kew Gardens in London.
● 1788: the first tuberous begonia, *Begonia octopetala*, arrived in Britian.
● 1789: Jonas Dryander, one of Sir Joseph Banks's curators, presented the results of his work, including 21 species of begonias, at the Linnaean Society.
Whereas a mere five species were being cultivated in Europe before 1800, the number increased rapidly after that. Famous botanists, politicians, plant collectors and travellers continued to discover new species of begonias on their expeditions and journeys and brought them back to Europe.
During the first half of the nineteenth century, it was mainly shrub and rhizomatous begonias that were cultivated in private and botanical gardens. Tuberous begonias and foliage begonias were almost unknown.

*A dahlia or a begonia?*
*The shape of the flower of the pendulous begonia "Blühwunder" is reminscent of a dahlia.*

*Rex begonias are indoor plants with extremely decorative leaves that require a quiet background for the best effect.*

### The very first begonia cultivars

The very earliest cultivars to be developed by gardeners and botanists who were keen on experimenting, were mainly shrub begonias. Many of these were created during the middle of the nineteenth century, for example:

● c. 1840 *Begonia* "Erythrophylla";
● c. 1847 *Begonia* "Ricinifolia";
● 1849 *Begonia* "Ingramii";
● 1855 *Begonia* "Verschaeffeltii".

After 1850 further important species were discovered which were to have a great and lasting influence on the future of begonia hybridizing.

### The creation of Rex begonias

In 1858, a Belgian company called Linden imported *Begonia rex* into Europe. Very soon, begonia experts realized the true potential of this rhizomatous begonia with its extremely colourful leaves, and they began to cross it with other species, for example, *Begonia imperialis* or *Begonia grandis*, a tuberous begonia which crosses surprisingly easily with foliage begonias. Finally, *Begonia diadema* brought bushier

growth, numerous smaller leaves and a little more elegance to the partnership. Its genes are still recognizable to this day. Rex begonias with Diadema begonia "blood" are characterized by deeply indented, jagged, longish leaves, while the classic Rex begonias have almost smooth-edged, more rounded leaves with a short tip. There are now so many cultivars that it is beyond the scope of this volume to describe them all. What they all have in common, however, is the enormous colour range of their leaves, which resemble complicated batik work (see photos, pp. 12/13). The flowers of Rex begonias are rather inconspicuous and play no part in their popularity.

## The creation of tuberous begonias

In the 1860s, great excitement was created among professional gardeners in Europe by the discovery of six tuberous begonia species in the Andes mountains of South America. Various hybridizing experiments were launched and the so-called tuber-hybrida group *(Begonia x tuber-hybrida)* was created. As this group involved particularly beautiful colours and shapes of flowers, species were used which supplied the following striking characteristics:

● *Begonia boliviensis*, a vivid shade of red;
● *Begonia rosiflora*, a deep pink;
● *Begonia pearcei*, a shade of yellow rare among tuberous begonias;
● *Begonia veitchii*, very large flowers and double flowers;
● *Begonia froebelii*, a profusion of flowers;
● *Begonia rosiflora*, via a certain seedling, white flowers;
● *Begonia davisii*, a great willingness to cross easily. This species was the basis for the Multiflora races. The results of all these hybridizing experiments were single- and double-flowering varieties with bearded, curly, fringed and striped petals in white, numerous shades of pink and red, yellow and orange.

During the 1870s and 1880s, tuberous begonias were so much in fashion that the most eminent plant raisers in Europe, such as Lemoine, Veitch and van Houtte, were kept very busy creating new hybrids. In Germany, Benary, Pfitzer and Diener made names for themselves. *Benary* produced such tuberous begonia classics as "Clips", "Memory", "Nonstop" and "Musical"

– F$_1$-hybrids which have won gold on about twenty occasions at diverse shows.

*Diener* introduced his romantic-looking rococo hybrids in 1981 – tuberous begonias with firm, beautifully curled flowers in vivid colours. He was also the creator of the striking turbo-F$_1$-hybrids with flowers that are 12 cm (4¼ in) long, in shades of yellow, salmon pink, pink, red and white, coupled with very dark foliage, or the "super begonias" whose gorgeous double flowers can be up to 16-20 cm (6¼-8 in) across. Youthful as ever is "Helene Harms", a yellow-flowering cultivar created in 1904. Still very popular and usually available are the old French hybrids like "Flamboyant" and "Mme Richard Galle". Last but not least, I must not forget to mention the single-flowering, compact, sun-loving "Bertiniis" (Bertinii-Compacta hybrids), which were created at the Benary nursery in the 1930s.

## The creation of hanging begonias

The experts' name for this group of tuberous begonias is *Begonia x tuberhybrida flore pleno pendula*. In 1890, the group was created in Belgium, originally having only small, single flowers in delicate colours. Then, from 1950 onwards, large-flowering forms were created that sported brilliant colours, for example, Pfitzer's "Elitenmischung", "Sonnenbegonie" or Benary's "Illumination Zartrosa".

## The creation of the Semperflorens begonias

The word "Semperflorens" is Latin and means ever-flowering. Originally, the name *Begonia semperflorens* (syn. *Begonia cuculata var. hookeri)* was given to an ever-green, semi-shrubby, wild species from Brazil, which flowers there from June to November, often even

longer. In 1829, a white variety of this species was brought to Europe. Interest in crossing this species was first shown in France. Victor Lemoine from Nancy was particularly successful, introducing the first red and large-flowering hybrids. Meanwhile, in Erfurt in Germany, Haage and Schmidt, as well as begonia raiser Benary, were also involved in Semperflorens hybridizing.

In those days it was the first, much more resistant *gracilis* forms and the *heterosis* varieties (representing the larger percentage of the selection that is available nowadays), introduced by Benary from 1909 onwards, which formed the milestones along the road to our modern cultivars. Of all begonia cultivars, Semperflorens begonias are the most widely available.

## The creation of Lorraine begonias

Lorraine begonias were created when the famous French plant raiser Lemoine crossed *Begonia socotrana* and *Begonia dregei* in 1891. He named these successful seedlings after his homeland of Lorraine by calling them "Gloire de Lorraine", a variety name which later became the name of a whole group of begonias. Numerous varieties had been created all over Europe by 1967, although, today, this group has been somewhat displaced by the more attractive Elatior and Rieger begonias and, currently, very few varieties are commonly available.

## The creation of the Elatior and Rieger begonias

Just like the Lorraine begonias, Elatior begonias have *Begonia socotrana* in their family tree. The first Elatior begonia was created in Britain in 1883, from *Begonia socotrana* crossed with various tuberous begonias.

*The leaves of Rex begonias display ever new, exciting patterns.*

*Red, black or silver are the preferred colours of these leafy beauties.*

Numerous strains (varieties) were created in Europe and America, many of which are not found anymore because the later Rieger and Elatior varieties were so successful. These later cultivars not only flower better but can also be propagated much more easily from leaf-cuttings than the early strains. Some of the well-known creations are: "Rieger's Aphrodite", "Rieger's Schwabenland" (see photo, p. 14), "Riegers Goldlachs", "Kolita", "Korona" (see photo, p. 14) and "Robella".

In the 1990s, after more than ten years of research, the begonia raisers of Benary managed to give Elatior begonias a new lease of life by creating "Charisma Coral" and "Charisma Orange" from seed. The truly exciting part of this is that these new varieties are the very first Elatior begonias ever that can be grown from seed.

## Varieties of foliage and shrub begonias

European raisers have been experimenting with these begonia groups too. Famous varieties include:
- "Argenteo-guttata" (see photo, p. 17), a cross between *Begonia albo-picta* and *Begonia olbia*;
- "Comte de Miribel" (see photo, p. 30), a cross between *Begonia coccinea* and *Begonia albo-picta*;
- "Lucerna" (see photo, p. 8), a Corallina hybrid;
- "Comtesse Louise Erdody", a cross between "Alexander von Humboldt" and *Begonia argentea-cupreata* (see photo, p. 19);
- "Bettina Rothschild", descendant of a Rex begonia (see photo, pp. 18/19);
- "Cleopatra", a foliage begonia cross between *Begonia* "Maphil" and *Begonia* "Black Beauty";
- Mexicross begonias, which have *Begonia boweri* and other foliage begonias in their family tree.

# Choosing the right varieties

Whether you wish to grow them indoors or in a conservatory, as a decorative plant for garden borders or in a tub on a patio, begonias come in a huge selection of colours, sizes and shapes at relatively low prices. They offer the opportunity to create beautiful flowerbeds, to collect rare varieties or simply to enjoy their beauty.

## How long do begonias last?

This depends on whether you are dealing with leafy begonias or shrub begonias, and on their position. Provided they receive the proper care, begonias in bright, temperature-regulated greenhouses or planted in beds will last longer than those planted in pots.

● Semperflorens, Elatior, Rieger and tuberous begonias are intended to be grown as annuals.

● Foliage and rhizomatous begonias tend to look unattractive in a pot after a certain time and will rarely last longer than two to three years.

● Shrub begonias, on the other hand, are exceptionally long-lived if given the right care. Fortunately, begonias belong to the type of plants that are extremely capable of regeneration, so it is fairly easy to propagate new plants from old ones (propagating, see pp. 38-41).

## A selection of available begonias

There are few countries in which one will find as many different, commonly available species and varieties of begonias as in the USA or France. Happily for begonia lovers in other places, more and more beautiful begonia varieties are now being imported. The following section introduces the most important groups.

## Semperflorens begonias

(photos and care, see pp. 22/23)
*Flowers:* white, white with pink edges, salmon pink, various shades of pink, red, single and double.
*Flowers* profusely.
Flowering time: from late spring until the first frosts.
*Size of flowers:* about 2 cm (¾ in).
*Foliage:* depending on the variety, blackish-red, green, rounded, gleams as if varnished.
*Height:* 15-45 cm (6-18 cm).
*Growth:* low, compact.
*Use:* in borders, boxes and pots. Low-growing varieties are used as groundcover in beds, as foreground plants in mixed planting and as effective cushions.
*Growth time:* annual.

*Special features:* undemanding, weather-hardy, can tolerate sunlight. There are low-growing and tall varieties, ones with large or small flowers and others with green or dark-coloured foliage.

## Tuberous begonias

(see photos and care, pp. 20/21)
*Flowers:* white, yellow, orange, pink, red, two-coloured, double.
*Flowering time:* from late spring to early frosts.
*Size of flowers:* 5-20 cm (2-8 in).
*Foliage:* pointed-oval, soft. Green, green and black marbled, slightly dentate edges; in the case of pendulous begonias, small, narrow and dark green.
*Height:* 30-50 cm (12-20 in).
*Growth:* compact, upright, round and bushy or overhanging.
*Use:* in boxes, large containers, borders and hanging baskets.
*Growth time:* annual. Some varieties can be made to shoot again the following year if the tubers are overwintered properly (see reviving the tuber, p. 36).
*The most important groups are:*
● Large-flowered Grandiflora hybrids with single, semi-double and double flowers. The flower is more than 10 cm (4 in) in diameter.
● Large-flowered Grandiflora-Compacta hybrids which grow fairly low and flower profusely and very early. Diameter of flowers, 8-10 cm (3¼-4in).
● Medium-sized flowering tuberous begonias with double and single flowers. Diameter of flowers, 6-10 cm (2¼-4 in).
● Small-flowering tuberous begonias which flower particularly profusely and are usually low-growing and bushy. Diameter of flowers, under 6 cm (2¼ in). Special feature: the Bertinii Compacta varieties can tolerate sunlight, grow slightly pendulously and look good in hanging baskets.

● Pendulous begonias with single, small or large flowers.

## Elatior begonias

(see photos and care, pp. 14/15) Originally, these were winter-flowering, but they are now sold for flowering all year round. This is made possible by artificially increasing or decreasing the daily amounts of light they receive. In plant nurseries the light supply can be controlled in this way to influence the growth of the plants and the development of their flowers.

**Flowers:** white, orange, salmon pink, pink, various shades of red, single and double.

**Flowering time:** all year, main flowering time from mid-winter to late spring.

**Size of flowers:** 2-3 cm (¾-1¼ in).

**Foliage:** Mid- to dark green, broad, slightly rounded, edges slightly jagged and wavy.

**Height:** about 30 cm (12 in).

**Growth:** luxuriant. The soft shoots will have to be supported by thin sticks, particularly when they bear flowers, unless you prefer the slightly pendulous nature of their growth and use the plants in a hanging basket.

**Suitable varieties:** "Aphrodite Radiant", "Aphrodite White" and "Aphrodite Red".

**Use:** indoor plant or in shady positions outside, sheltered from the wind.

**Growth time:** annual.

## Lorraine begonias

Very few specimens from this group are still on the market today.

**Flowers:** white, white/pink, various shades of pink, single, the stamens are often a vivid yellow.

**Flowering time:** late autumn.

**Size of flowers:** 2-3 cm (¾-1¼ in).

**Foliage:** rounded, green or red.

**Height:** about 20 cm (8 in).

**Growth:** low-growing, compact,

*Shrub begonia "Comte de Miribel" growing outside in summer.*

almost spherical. Shoots like Elatior and Rieger begonias.
*Use:* decorative indoor plant.
*Growth time:* annual.

## Foliage begonias

(see photos and care, pp. 21/13)
*Flowers:* rather inconspicuous in many species and varieties.
*Foliage:* attractive and very varied depending on species and varieties.
*Height:* 25-100 cm (10-40 in).
*Growth:* upright or slightly to very pendulous.
*Use:* on windowsills, picture windows, for hanging baskets, on pedestals.
*Growth time:* annual and perennial. The most popular, commonly available varieties are:
● *Begonia rex* hybrids, of which there are now numerous, breathtakingly beautiful varieties.
● *Begonia masoniana* "Iron Cross".
● *Begonia boweri* hybrids like *var. nigramarga* with small leaves that have bristles along their edges; 15-20 cm tall (6-8 in).
● Mexicross begonias, which look similar to *nigramarga* and whose ancestors were *Begonia boweri*, *Begonia heracleifolia*, *Begonia mazae* and *Begonia smaragdina*.
● *Begonia diadema*, with leaves that are 15-25 cm (6-10 in) long, broadly oval in shape, with white spots. Pink flowers in spring.
● *Begonia heracleifolia*. This species is remarkable for its thick, often upright rhizome. The leaves have seven to nine indentations, are hand-shaped, dark or moss green, and have lighter coloured markings. In addition, there are varieties with blackish-green markings and red leaf undersides (example, *Begonia heracleifolia var. nigricans*). Pink flowers in spring (see photo, p. 19). Similar: *Begonia x ricinifolia*.
● *Begonia imperialis*, with 10 cm (4 in) almost circular leaves with a silky sheen.

## Shrub begonias

(photos and care, see pp. 16/17)
*Flowers:* various, depending on the species or variety.
*Foliage:* various, as above.
*Height:* 20-200 cm (8-80 in).
*Growth:* upright, climbing, pendulous, with thin or thick shoots.
*Use:* in large containers or pots, or in a hanging basket.
*Growth time:* perennial.
The following are the most important representatives:
● Corallina hybrids. They form shoots up to 2 m (80 in) long, become woody later on and bear nodding, false umbels in various shades of red all year round. Best known variety: "Lucerna" (see photo, p. 8).
● *Begonia limmingheana* (syn. *Begonia procumbens*). Flowers from early to late spring in a flood of delicate pink to coral red flowers. The leaves are almost heart-shaped and slightly wavy along the edges. Pendulous plant.
● *Begonia serratipetala* has pink flowers from spring to autumn and features red foliage. Looks best in a hanging basket where the sunlight can shine through the red leaves and make them glow. 30-45 cm (12-18 in) high.
● *Begonia foliosa var. miniata* (the fuchsia begonia) forms luxuriant inflorescences from mid-winter to mid-spring in colours ranging from scarlet to light pink and coral. Grows upright and branches profusely. Attractive variety: "Corbeille du Feu", with a tall stem and coral red flowers and small, light green, rounded leaves.
● *Begonia "Argenteo-guttata"*. Grows in a semi-shrub shape and will attain a height of 1 m (40 in). Pendulous inflorescences with large, white and red flowers. The leaves are patterned with white spots (see photo, p. 17).
● *Begonia metallica* flowers from

early autumn in a deep shade of pink and will grow to about 100 cm (40 in). The olive green leaves have a metallic sheen and deep-seated purple-red veins. The flowers are covered in prickly reddish-pink hairs (see photo, p. 16).
● *Begonia "Sachsen"* is a real "beginner's" begonia which flowers profusely.
● *Begonia egregia*. A species with vigorous shoots and silvery green, extremely hairy foliage, and which bears white flowers in winter (see photo, p. 17).
● *Begonia "Manuela"* flowers in the summer and has a scent that resembles that of an orchid (see photo, p. 17).
● *Begonia "Amazing Lace"* has white flowers and interesting, jagged foliage (see photo, p. 17).

## Begonias for collectors

(photos and care, see pp. 18/19)
If you wish to grow any of these less-common varieties, you will have to seek out a specialist nursery. Your local garden centre should be able to supply an address.

## Where to buy begonias

*Tubers* for starting tuberous begonias can be obtained in spring, and also sometimes from late winter onwards, in garden centres, specialist flower shops, through mail order or from specialist nurseries.
*Ready-grown tuberous begonias, pendulous begonias and Semperflorens begonias* can be found from mid-spring to late summer on market stalls, in flower shops, garden centres, nurseries and some supermarkets.
*NB:* None of these plants can tolerate freezing temperatures. Plants bought in tubs should not be placed outside if frosts are still to be expected! Do not plant Semperflorens begonias until after the last frosts of late spring.

*Elatior begonias and foliage begonias* can be purchased in specialist flower shops, nurseries, flower markets, supermarkets and garden centres. The main season for flowering begonias is from early winter to late spring, but foliage begonias can be obtained all year round. *Shrub begonias* can be bought in garden centres, specialist plant shops and, occasionally, in supermarkets. If you are looking for something special, however, it is probably better to try a specialist

nursery (your local garden centre should be able to give you an address).

*Rare begonias* can usually only be obtained from specialist nurseries (ask at your garden centre).
*NB:* Begonias are extremely sensitive to cold and can only be sent by mail order during the frost-free months of the year.

## What to look for when buying begonias

No matter which species or variety they belong to, as a rule begonias are rather easy to damage as they have fairly brittle stems. These do, however, tend to regenerate themselves quite quickly. Even so, it is a good idea to check when buying that:
● the flowers and leaves do not have brown spots or edges;
● the leaves are free of mildew;
● the shoots look firm and healthy;
● the rootstock is not dried up.

## Care of begonias that arrive by post

Botanical rarities and shrub begonias, in particular, are usually sent by post. As a rule, you will receive young plants which have been well packed, to avoid broken or bent shoots. They will recover from their journey fairly rapidly if they are immediately placed in a warm, bright position (not sunny) and the soil around them is kept moist. It will be unnecessary to buy more expensive, larger plants as the young plants should adapt well to their new conditions and should grow a great deal bigger during their first year.

**My tip:** If the mail order plants do arrive with bent or broken shoots, cut off the relevant shoot with a clean, sharp knife and disinfect the cut surface with charcoal powder.

Then, just push the cut-off shoot into compost. In a few weeks' time, the shoot will form new roots.

## Begonias indoors

Begonias are excellent subjects if you wish to create an interesting arrangement of plants. They are suitable:
● as neighbours for exotic plant combinations in a window;
● for planting in hanging baskets and shallow bowls;
● for making a row of decorative, colourful plants on a windowsill;
● as an eye-catching feature when placed on a pedestal;
● as a colourful table arrangement;
● as large container plants or in hanging baskets for balconies that are sheltered from the wind.

## Suitable pot holders

Begonias have their own characteristic shades and interesting patterns so it is a good idea to use simple pot holders in a single colour. If you wish, you can, of course, choose pots with patterns and colours that echo those of the plants; this can result in quite a sophisticated effect. Always make sure that the pot holder does not fit too snugly around the flowerpot, so that plenty of air can circulate. Even if you cannot see it, any surplus water must be poured away so that the plant does not suffer damage through waterlogging!

## Hydroponically grown begonias

The best results have been obtained with Rex begonias. Current experiments with shrub begonias seem to be yielding promising results. No results are yet available for tuberous begonias. It might be worth while trying to grow them in Hortag, Perlite or some other synthetic soil.

**My tip:** Only use the hydroponic method with begonias that you have

---

**Suitable species and varieties for indoors**
*For a warm, humid plant-display window:* Rex hybrids and other rhizomatous begonias.
*For pedestals and hanging baskets:* Begonia foliosa, Begonia limmingheana, Begonia masoniana, Begonia mazae, Begonia scandens (syn. Begonia glabra), Begonia solananthera, Begonia "Weisser Ehane", Corallina hybrids.
*Begonias which remain small and are therefore suitable for shallow bowls:* Begonia boweri, Begonia goegoensis, Begonia imperialis and their varieties.
*Easy-to-care-for begonias for beginners:* Begonia "Argenteo-guttata", Begonia coccinea, Begonia "Corbeille de Feu", Begonia "Credneri", Begonia "Erythrophylla", Begonia "Lucerna", Begonia metallica, Begonia "Mrs Fred Scrips", Begonia "Sachsen".
*Scented begonias:* Begonia "Bettina Rothschild", Begonia dichroa, Begonia egregia, Begonia "Joe Hayden", Begonia "Manuela", Begonia "Richmondensis", Begonia solananthera, Begonia venosa.

*Green and white variegated foliage offers a charming contrast to these coral red Semperflorens begonias.*

grown successfully as cuttings and which have actually formed roots in fine Hortag and a hydro-nutrient solution. Trying to transfer plants that were raised in compost to a hydroponic environment is extremely difficult and probably doomed to failure.

### Begonias in the garden
It is a fact that the brilliant colours of tuberous begonias do not stand competition from other species of plants. A very attractive combination is to plant red and white pendulous begonias together in a large hanging basket. Semperflorens begonias are most effective as a carpet combining two or three varying shades.

**My tip:** If you live near the sea or in an area where grapes are grown, you can plant *Begonia grandis evansiana* outside. This tuberous begonia, which originated in China, will become dormant if the temperature drops below freezing. It is extremely attractive in a rockery and can tolerate direct sunlight.

### Begonias for balcony or patio
The same species can be used as in the garden. Especially recommended are the tuberous begonias which do not need much room. You can even try growing shrub begonias on balconies sheltered from the wind, rain and sun, as they usually flower in the summer and flourish in warm, moist air, but do not place them outside until the beginning of summer! Lorraine and Elatior begonias can also go outside from the middle of the last month of spring onwards.

# Planting, care and propagating

As they were originally tropical forest dwellers, most begonias are used to plenty of warmth, shade, high humidity and water-permeable soil. We have to try to reproduce these ideal conditions as best we can in order to make our plants feel at home in a temperate climate.

## Light requirements

Whether they are grown indoors or in a garden, and no matter which species or variety we are dealing with, begonias do best in bright positions but not in direct sunlight. East- or west-facing positions are particularly favourable. During the winter, however, begonias kept indoors will be quite grateful for a few hours of sunshine. Only Semperflorens and the tuberous begonias of the Bertinii-Compacta group can tolerate full sunlight and even they should not be subjected to bright, direct sunlight in a hot position with little air movement.

**My tip:** It is a mistake to look upon begonias as purely shade-loving plants. I have found from experience that shrub begonias, particularly the ones with bamboo-like shoots, need plenty of light in order to flower profusely and not grow lanky, and so that their foliage will develop the right colours.

## Temperature

The right temperature will depend on the requirements of the individual species and varieties. During their main growth period, all begonias need plenty of warmth. It is particularly important during the winter months that the soil remains warm enough. To prevent your indoor begonias from getting "cold feet" on chilly windowsills, insulation can be provided in the form of polystyrene sheets, or an electric heating mat can be used.
*Important:* Fresh air but no draughts!

## Humidity

The ideal range of humidity for begonias is somewhere between 40 and 60%. A higher amount should be avoided as this would bring the danger of decay, while a lower amount would lead to leaf edges curling up and becoming brown or to falling leaves.

**My tip:** Even though begonias like humid air, never spray the leaves. Make sure that humid air is provided by an indirect source. Electric humidifiers etc. can be employed or you could stand your begonia pot in a larger pot and fill the space between the pots with moist peat, Hortag or some similar medium. (This should only be done if the plant is in a clay pot.)

## The right soil

The soil should be loose, well aerated, water-permeable, contain nutrients and be peat-based rather than containing a lot of lime.
Good begonia soils are:
● peat-based soil;
● standard soil, consisting of 60% moss peat and 40% loam, already enriched with nutrients;
● all commercial, ready-mixed, flower potting composts, but make sure they are of good quality!

## Repotting

You should not repot begonias as a matter of course in spring, only when necessary, if:
● the rootstock has become matted;
● the plant is not growing well or looks sickly;
● the plant has grown so much that the container and plant parts above ground appear out of balance. Some shrub begonias grow so vigorously that they have to be repotted three times in one year using new compost and a larger pot.

**My tip:** When repotting, mix polystyrene flakes or Perlite with the new compost or soil. This will make it even looser.

## The golden rules of watering

Take a good look at a begonia. It has succulent stems, sap-filled leaves and produces vigorous growth – by its very nature, a plant like that will need plenty of water.

*"Sunshine" on your windowsill*
*Orange and golden yellow Elatior begonias will create a cheerful display.*

The rootstock of a begonia should never be allowed to dry up. On the other hand, "wet feet" and floods of water are not required either:

● It is better to water less often, but thoroughly, than often and superficially!

● Always get rid of surplus water so that the roots do not cool down too much and start decaying.

● Use soft water at room temperature, or sun-warmed water.

● Alternately water from the top and from below, so that the nutrient salts can be absorbed in a balanced way.

● Try to water the soil only, not the leaves, to avoid fungal and bacterial infections.

● Make sure there is adequate drainage. Waterlogging is lethal for begonias!

● Water in the mornings so that the soil has a chance to dry by the evening when it is cooler.

● Never water outside begonias during the hours around midday or in full sunlight.

● Pendulous begonias and/or begonias in hanging baskets will dry out rapidly on warm summer days or in heated rooms. I recommend taking them down and watering them thoroughly every day.

## Fertilizing

The nutrients to which begonias have access in a pot will only last for a limited period. The time and frequency of fertilizing is described in the plan of care for each individual group (see pp. 10-23). As a rule :

● It is better to give small doses often than high doses occasionally. The fine root systems of begonias react sensitively to nutrient salts. Half of the amount of fertilizer recommended on the packet per litre of water will be sufficient.

● Only fertilize the plant during its main growth phase when it is obviously growing.

● Do not fertilize dry soil.

● After repotting, wait for three weeks before fertilizing again.

● Never allow fertilizer solution to run on to the leaves as this may cause burns!

*Suitable fertilizers:* Mineral compound and special fertilizers which can be obtained in liquid or powdered form. They contain the main nutrients required for the plant's growth: nitrogen (N), phosporous (P) and potassium (K), as well as trace elements in a ratio suitable for the plant. Controlled-release fertilizers are also suitable and are commercially available in the form of granules, fertilizer sticks or cones.

**My tip:** Begonias particularly need calcium (lime) and potassium for strengthening their tissues, which contain a large percentage of water. I add kaolin to the water every four weeks (1 tsp to every litre/1¾ pt of water).

## Reviving tuberous begonias

The tubers of these begonias can be overwintered and then revived so that they will flower again, but this can only be done for about two or three years, after when the plant will become increasingly weak.

*Method*

● The tubers (bought or overwintered) are laid close together, side by side, in a box full of moist peat in late winter/early spring. Put the box in a place where the temperature is 18-20°C (64-69°F). The depression or hollow in the tuber should be facing upwards.

● As soon as new shoots are visible, plant the tubers individually in large pots or in their final container (boxes, bowls, pots, etc.). Mix a controlled-release fertilizer with the compost. If the depression at the top of the tuber is clearly visible from the start, you can place the tuber in its final container right away.

● Cover the shooting tubers with a layer of soil about one finger's width deep.

● Keep the soil moist by spraying it regularly.

● As soon as leaves have formed, take the boxes or pots outside to toughen up the plants. Protect the plants from frost!

● Plant them out in a bed from the middle of the last month of spring, having first worked some compound fertilizer into the soil. Improve heavy soils with sand and hygromulch.

## Begonias do not like:

● stagnant air
● draughts
● gas
● spray for making leaves shine
● plant protection agents
● dry air
● too much humidity
● blows or pressure
● waterlogging
● water on their leaves and flowers
● dense soil
● a dark position in winter
● direct sunlight
● too much fertilizer
● "cold feet"

## Pests and diseases

Many begonias have fleshy, succulent stems and delicate leaves which can easily be infected by fungi, viruses or bacteria. From experience, it is known that if the tubers of tuberous begonias are cut or damaged, they can easily start to decay and, in some cases, may even die. Unfortunately, begonias (particularly when flowering) cannot tolerate almost any type of plant protection agent. The best preventive measure is good care, an optimal position and to propagate new plants while the parent plant is still healthy.

# Diseases, pests and forms of treatment

| Symptoms | Cause | Treatment |
|---|---|---|
| Rolled-up leaves, dried-up edges | Position too warm or too dry | Water the plant and place it in a cooler spot. |
| Loss of leaves in winter | Position too cool | Place the plant in a brighter and warmer position; in particular, provide the soil with warmth |
| Decaying stems | Too much watering | Allow the soil to dry. Then, water less frequently but more thoroughly. Get rid of surplus water |
| Visible decay of leaves, flowers and flowerbuds | Spraying | Do not wet the plant when watering |
| Yellow, weak leaves | Position too cold and wet | Do not continue watering until the plant has recovered. Make sure the roots and soil are kept warmer |
| Leaves that remain small, no flowers | Lack of nutrients | Fertilize |
| Flowers and buds dropping off | Indoor air too dry, position too dark | Supply the plant with more light and indirect humidity (see p. 34) |
| Red discoloration of leaf edges | Position too sunny, lack of nitrogen and calcium | Stand the plant in a bright, but not sunny, position and fertilize it regularly during its growth period |
| Pale leaves | Lack of iron, "cold feet" | Stand the plant in a place where the soil and roots will be warm enough, and water with softened water containing an iron preparation Repot in the spring |
| Crippled or deformed leaves, cork-like spots on leaf stalks, stems and the undersides of leaves | Cyclamen mites | Remove infested parts. Keep the plant drier and cooler |
| Discoloured leaves | Leaf-blotch eelworms | Remove infested parts. Do not allow the leaves to become wet when watering |
| Yellow spots on leaves. Fine web-like structures on undersides of leaves | Spider mites | Place the plant in a transparent plastic bag for 1-2 days. Water beforehand |
| Rusty brown spots along the ribs of leaves | Infestation with thrips, caused by the surrounding air being too dry | Remove infested leaves. Spray the plant with an insecticide recommended against thrips. Or set up a bio-friendly greenhouse fly catcher strip or some similar device in or around the pot. Make sure humidity is increased (see p. 34) |
| Yellowed, dried-up leaves, unnatural growths on the roots | Bacterial infection | Not possible. There is a danger of other begonias becoming infected. Destroy the plant |
| Glassy "oil spots" on uppersides of leaves | Bacterial "oil patch" disease, which can be caused by wetting the leaves when watering | Not possible. There is a danger of other begonias becoming infected. Destroy the plant |
| Deformed leaves with yellow rings and spots | Viral infection | Not possible. There is a danger of other begonias becoming infected. Destroy the plant |
| Greyish-brown, mealy spots on leaves and shoots, leaves dying | Grey mould caused by too much moisture and stagnant air | Remove infected leaves. Stand the plant in a drier, airier place and spray it with a fungicide |
| A white, powdery layer on leaves and shoots | Mildew | Treat as for grey mould |

# Propagating

At some time or another, nearly every begonia enthusiast will wish to grow some new plants, either to obtain more specimens of a particular favourite or to have extra plants to give away to other plant lovers. The good thing about begonias is that they are endowed with enormous regenerative faculties and can be propagated in various different ways. Most of them are propagated by the vegetative method, by using parts of the parent plant. This is also the most successful method for amateur plant growers as you are guaranteed to obtain specimens that are practically identical to the parent plant. The following parts of plants are suitable for use in propagating: tips of shoots, leaf sections, leaves, leaf cuttings, parts of rhizomes and cuttings from tubers.

## Propagating equipment
● completely healthy parent plants;
● a clean pair of secateurs or a sharp, disinfected knife;
● charcoal powder for disinfecting the cut surfaces;
● rooting powder;
● small pots made of clay or plastic, and seed trays or propagating dishes;
● plastic bags;
● thick flower wire;
● a plate of glass for covering the propagating dishes;
● name tags for recording the name of the parent plant and the propagation date;
● a propagating bed that can be heated, or a heating mat. Warm soil is enormously important for root formation.

## Good propagating compost
All begonias need a compost that is well aerated and water-permeable.

The following examples are suitable:
● a mixture of seeding compost and Perlite in equal parts;
● a mixture of peat, sand and Perlite in equal parts;
● a mixture of vermiculite, Perlite and peat or sand in equal parts.

Special composts can be obtained in the gardening trade or through mail order.

1. Cut off a shoot tip with at least two sets of healthy leaves.

3. Remove the lowest set of leaves and pinch out the buds and flowers.

5. Push the cutting into potting compost and press it down lightly.

## Propagating at the right time
The spring months are particularly favourable for vegetative propagation. If you can provide the optimal lighting conditions by using artificial lighting, so much the better, as you can then continue propagating into the first month of autumn.

## Propagating from shoot tips
Take cuttings of young shoot tips,

2. Cut the stem cleanly immediately below a set of leaves.

4. Allow the cut surface to dry, then dip it in rooting powder.

6. Water, then insert two arched wires and pull a plastic bag over them.

which should be 8-10 cm (3¼-4 in) long and have at least two sets of healthy leaves.

**Rooting in water:** Stand the cuttings in a glass of water in a bright, warm place. As soon as strong roots have formed, the small plants can be potted.

**Rooting in soil** (see illustrations 1-6 on p. 38): Roots are formed after about three to four weeks.

**Important:** You must provide a bright position which affords plenty of warmth for the soil and humid air, which can be provided by means of a transparent plastic bag. Remove the bag for five minutes daily to prevent decay. Once the roots have grown, remove the bag completely.

**My tip:** In the case of large-leaved species and varieties, split the leaf in half. This will reduce the surface of the leaf, prevent drying out through evaporation and the cutting will find it easier to develop roots.

## Propagating from leaf section cuttings

Both methods are equally successful if the following requirements are met:
● warm compost;
● constantly slightly moist, but never wet, compost;
● humid air (see above). Do not forget to air the plastic bag daily.

**Propagating from a leaf in which slits have been cut across the rib** (see illustrations 1-3, right).
1. Remove a healthy, vigorous leaf from the parent plant, turn it underside up on a wooden board and cut slits in the leaf, through the veins below each branch.
2. Lay the leaf, with the incisions downwards, on compost and weigh it down with stones to ensure an even contact with the compost.
3. Keep the compost moist and warm by pulling a transparent plastic bag over the tray or lying a plate

of glass on top. Tiny new plants will grow out of the incisions.

**Propagating from parts of leaves** (see illustrations 4-6, right column): This is a particularly good method if the parent plant has very large leaves and if you need lots of new plants from the one parent plant.
4. Cut the leaf down in size (so that the width across the central vein is about 5 cm/2 in), using a sharp

knife. Remove the leaf stalk.
5. Cut out individual leaf segments, each of which must still retain a portion of the central vein.
6. Push these segments, with the edge that was nearest to the leaf stalk downwards, into slightly moist propagating compost. Cover the tray with a plastic bag or a plate of glass and place it in a bright, warm position.

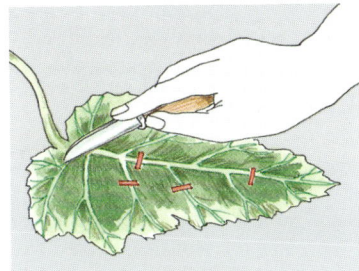

*1. Make small incisions in the larger veins just below each branch.*

*4. Remove the leaf stalk. Cut away some of the leaf on each side.*

*2. Weigh the leaf down so that the incisions touch the compost.*

*5. Cut the leaf into segments that are about 5 cm (2 in) long.*

*3. Keep the compost moist and warm. Tiny plants will appear.*

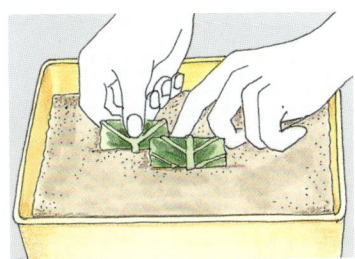

*6. Push the segments into compost with the direction of growth upwards.*

# Propagating

## Propagating from leaves

Propagating from individual leaves is particularly suitable for small-leaved species and varieties, for example, *Begonia boweri*. For this purpose, cut off the leaves, together with their stalks, and insert the stalk in compost.

*Important:* The surface of the leaf must not be allowed to touch the compost as this would bring a risk of decay, so make sure that the stalk is long enough to avoid this.

## Propagating from leaf cuttings

This method is often used with shrub begonias. A long shoot is cut up into various pieces, each of which must retain at least two leaves. This means that you will need a shoot with plenty of side shoots. Propagating is carried out in the same way as for shoot tip cuttings (see p. 39). The difference here is that the cuttings should not be pushed as deeply into the soil as with the shoot tip method. The rooting time is three to four weeks. You can tell if rooting has been success-ful when new shoots and leaves form on the young plant. When this happens, remove the plastic bag.

## Propagating by dividing the rhizome

(see illustration below)
This is the ideal method of propagation for rhizomatous begonias, and the Rex hybrids in particular. The method is very successful and will produce strong and flourishing plants within a very short period of time. In addition, the new begonias are usually much more attractive than the parent plants, as older rhizomatous begonias often become unsightly in time. Depending on the species, the rhizomes may be thick or thin, prostrate or upright. The most important points for success-ful propagating (particularly for thicker rhizomes) are a clean cut and the strictest hygiene as a large cut surface offers ideal conditions for invasion by bacteria and fungi. Always make sure to dip your knife in a plant disinfectant or alcohol before making the cut.

### Method

● Both the tip of the rhizome and the central section are equally suit-able for propagating. Cut off the rhi-zome in such a way that each sec-tion has at least one set of two leaves.

● Allow the cut surface to dry, then dip it in rooting powder.

● The position of the rhizome on the parent plant should be copied when the cutting is placed in the compost. This means setting upright rhizome sections upright in the compost and setting prostrate parts horizontally in the compost.

● Pull a plastic bag over the pot and leave it there until the roots have formed, or cover the propagating container with a plate of glass or a hood. Stand the propagating container in a bright, warm position and air it daily! The rooting time is about four weeks. Do not forget to remove the plastic bag or other cover after the young plant has rooted successfully.

## Propagating from tiny tubers

These small tubers are formed by some begonias (for example, *Begonia gracilis*, *Begonia grandis* and others) in the leaf axils during the autumn and are eminently suit-able for propagating.
Remove the tiny tubers as soon as the main plant starts dying back

*1. If the rhizome is growing over the edge of the pot, it can be cut off and used for propagating.*

*2. Cut segments of the rhizome in such a way that there is always at least one leaf and one node per segment.*

above ground. Store the small tubers in a dry place at 13°C (55°F) during the winter. In the spring, plant them separately in pots, so that they are barely covered with soil, and stand them in a bright, warm position, keeping the soil slightly moist.

The little tubers will take four to six weeks to form roots. The plants will reach their full size during their second year and flower then for the first time.

## Propagating by dividing the main tuber

(see illustrations 1-4, right)
This method is only suitable for thick tubers packed with nutrients. Tubers which do not appear to have increased at all by the spring (compared to their size before the winter) or seem lacking in energy will not have enough stength to survive the procedure. This also goes for semi-tuberous species which are better propagated by shoot tip cuttings (see p. 39). To help you to find the right places to cut the tubers, you must encourage them to revive.

### Method

1. Newly bought or overwintered tubers are bedded in a small box of moistened, loose peat, thinly covered with a layer of moist compost, then placed in a warm (18-20° C/64-68°F) bright position.
2. As soon as the shoot buds start appearing, cut the tuber in sections. *Important:* each segment must have one shoot bud.
Leave the cut surfaces to dry in the air for a few hours, then dip them in charcoal powder to prevent decay.
3. Place the segments in individual pots or boxes.
4. If they have been planted together in small boxes, separate them later on and plant them in individual pots, at the latest, when the young plants start touching each other. The new young plants will not be as

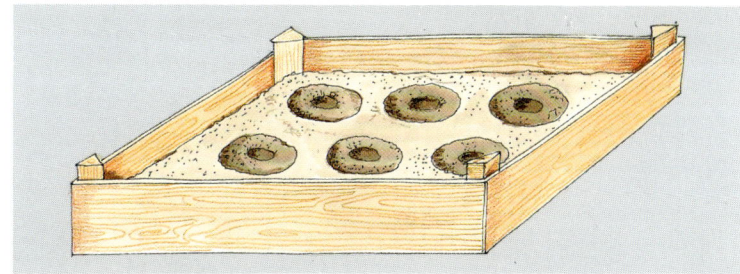

1. To revive the tubers, bed them, with the hollow uppermost, in a small flat box of moistened peat. Cover them with a thin layer of compost.

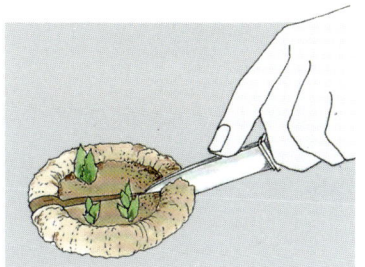

2. Cut the tubers into segments, each of which retains one shoot.

3. Allow the segments to dry, then place them in pots or boxes.

4. Make sure to transplant them to individual pots before they grow too close together. Mix controlled-release fertilizer with the new compost.

robust as undivided specimens but they will rapidly make up for this by the summer. The tuber will grow larger but will retain the shape of the cut segment.

### Further growth

If you want to obtain bushy growth, you should occasionally pinch out the shoot tips of the young plants. As soon as the young begonia

threatens to outgrow the confines of its pot, it is time to repot it (see p. 34). It should be watered well and fertilized, depending on what is recommended for each species or variety (see pp. 10-23).

### Propagating from seed

This method is very difficult for the layperson and is not recommended.

## Additional tips for shrub begonias

Some shrub begonias need further care because they grow so tall.

*Support sticks:* All begonias that grow upright with relatively soft, fragile stems, as well as those that flower profusely or become very tall, should be supported with sticks. Start to supply these while the plants are still quite young. Each shoot should be tied individually to the support. When repotting, try to keep the sticks in position or replace them with stronger, taller ones if they have become too short or thin for the plant. In time, the begonia will cover up the ties with plenty of foliage.

*Cutting back and pinching out shoots:* People often wonder if shrub begonias should be pruned. Generally speaking this is not necessary. Unfortunately, however, some species grow so vigorously that a corrective pruning of unruly shoots will be called for. It is important to cut out any old wood so that the plant has room for new shoots. If shrub begonias begin to look lanky, they can be cut right back to five sets of leaves per shoot. They will shoot again quickly and grow bushier than before. Another advantage of cutting back is that you can use cut-off pieces for propagating purposes (see p. 39).

*A collector's delight*
*This windowsill contains a treasure trove of foliage and shrub begonias. As shown in the top left corner of the photograph, shrub begonias will require some kind of support to hold up the heavy blossoms.*

# Index

Figures given in bold indicate illustrations.

# Index

## A begonia museum

The largest begonia collection to date can be seen in the French town of Rochefort-sur-Mer, Michel Bégon's home town. In this "museum", which is really a working research institute with an area of 600 sq m (718 sq yd) under glass, 450 different species and hybrids, among them both old and forgotten and newly discovered begonias, are grown. The greenhouse is open to the public on Tuesday and Thursday afternoons for a maximum of two guided tours. An appointment will be necessary. The address is: Serre Conservatoire Begonia de Rochefort "La Prée Horticole", 21 rue Charles Plumier, F-17300 Rochefort, France.

*Important:* The best way of finding the address of your nearest begonia society, specialist nursery, etc. is to enquire at your local garden centre. For a small fee, specialist nurseries will usually send a catalogue detailing their selection of available plants, specialities and conditions of purchase.

### Important note

This book covers the care of begonias for indoors, on balconies and patios or in the garden. To date, no cases of poisoning from ingesting parts of begonia plants are known (see p. 9), but I still strongly recommend that you make sure that children and animals are not able to consume any parts of begonia plants.

*Flowering splendour in the shade*
*Tuberous begonias produce a veritable*
*firework display of colour in the summer*
*and will make even a shady garden bed*
*glow with light. They look particularly*
*attractive in front of a sedate background*
*of shrubs and trees.*

**Cover photographs:**
Front cover main picture: *Begonia*
semperflorens; top right: *Begonia 'Alpha*
*Scarlet'*; middle right: *Stunning, double-*
*flowered Begonia pendula*; bottom right:
*Begonia 'Apricot Delight'.*
Inside front cover: *Various foliage begonias.*
Inside back cover: *A cheerful, colourful*
*border of tuberous begonias.*
Back cover: *Tuberous begonias.*

**Photographic acknowledgements**
BAMBOO/Descat: 17 bottom right, 18,
19 top right; Benary: 14 top right,
21 bottom left, 22; John Glover, Garden
Picture Library: front cover top right;
Heitz: 17 top left; Mein Schöner
Garten/Graham: 21 middle, left, top right;
Mein Schöner Garten/Wolff: 21 top left,
bottom right; Reinhard: 23; Rose: 8, 10;
H.S. Sira, Garden Picture Library: front
cover middle right and bottom right;
Strauss: 30, 33; Graham Strong: front
cover main picture, back cover; Welsch:
26, 29; Stork: all other photographs.

This edition published 1999 by
Merehurst Limited
Ferry House, 51–57 Lacy Road,
Putney, London SW15 1PR

© 1989 Gräfe und Unzer GmbH, Munich

ISBN 1-85391-719-2

English text copyright ©
Merehurst Limited 1994
*Translated by* Astrid Mick
*Edited by* Lesley Young
*Design/typesetting by* Cooper Wilson Design
*Illustrations by* Ushie Dorner
*Printed in Hong Kong* by Wing King Tong